ANN ROSSI

CULTURES COLLIDE

Native Americans and Europeans
1492–1700

NATIONAL GEOGRAPHIC
Washington, D.C.

PICTURE CREDITS: Front Cover Francis G. Mayor/CORBIS; p. 1 The Bridgeman Art Library; pp. 2–3 L.K. Townsend, National Geographic Society; pp. 5, 6, 10, 13, 21, 27, 29, 30, 33, (straw motif) Gunter Marx/CORBIS; pp. 4–5, 6 (top) 7, 9 (top), 10, 10, 16, 21 (top), 26, 27 (top), 29 (top), 30, 33 (top), 36-37, 39 Library of Congress; p. 6 John Berkey; pp. 8–9 Jack Parsons; pp. 10–11 Richard Schlecht; p. 12 Granger Collection, NY; p. 14 David A. Harvey; p. 15 Rochester Museum & Science Center; pp. 16 (inset), 17 (inset) K.T. Design; pp. 18, 27 Photograph courtesy of the Royal Ontario Museum; pp. 20, 22 Terry Eiler; p. 21 Dick S. Durrance/National Geographic Society, Image Collection; pp. 23, 31 North Wind Picture Archives; p. 24 Arthur Lidov; p. 25 Carl F. Wimar, *The Buffalo Hunt*, 1860. Oil on canvas, 35 1/4" x 60", Washington University Gallery of Art, St. Louis. Gift of Dr. William Van Zandt, 1886; p. 28 (left & bkgd.) Otis Imboden,Jr./National Geographic Society, Image Collection; p. 28 (center) Bruce A. Dale/National Geographic Society, Image Collection; pp. 28 (right), 35 Joseph H. Bailey/National Geographic Society, Image Collection; p. 29 (bottom) Wolfgang Bayer/Bruce Coleman, Inc., NY, p. 32 Culver Pictures, Inc., NY; p. 33 Philip Schermeister/National Geographic Society, Image Collection; pp. 34, 40 Medford Taylor/National Geographic Society, Image Collection; p. 34 (inset) Paul M. Breeden; p. 38 Burgess Blevins/FP; MAPS: p.7, Equator Graphics; p. 17, K. T. Design

QUOTATIONS: P. 4 From *Seeds of Change*, edited by Herman J. Viola and Carolyn Margolis (Washington, D.C.: Smithsonian Institution Press, 1991); p. 12; p. 7, From *The European Challenge* (Alexandria, VA: Time-Life Books, 1992), p. 9; p. 15, From *500 Nations, An Illustrated History of North American Indians*, by Alvin M. Josephy, Jr. (NY: Alfred A. Knopf, 1994), p. 47; p. 22, From *After Columbus: The Smithsonian Chronicle of the North American Indians*, by Herman J. Viola (Washington, D.C.: Smithsonian Institution Press, 1990), p. 65; p. 31, From *After Columbus: The Smithsonian Chronicle of the North American Indians*, p. 59; p. 38, From *American Indian Science: A New Look At Old Cultures* (NY: Twenty-First Century Books, 1997), p. 9.

Library of Congress Cataloging-in-Publication Data

Rossi, Ann.
   Cultures collide: Native Americans and Europeans, 1492–1700 / by Ann Rossi.
      v. cm. — (*Crossroads America*)
      ISBN: 0-7922-7189-0
Contents: Different cultures, different ways—New harvests, new foods —The horse: changing lifestyles—Trade—Changing ways of life. 1. Indians of North America—First contact with Europeans—Juvenile literature. 2. Indians of North America—Social life and customs—Juvenile literature. 3. America—Discovery and exploration—Juvenile literature. [1. Indians of North America—History. 2. America—Discovery and exploration.] I. Title. II. Series. Includes index.
   E98.F39R67 2004
   970.01—dc22

                        2003018432

Produced through the worldwide resources of the National Geographic Society, John M. Fahey, Jr., President and Chief Executive Officer; Gilbert M. Grosvenor, Chairman of the Board; Nina D. Hoffman, Executive Vice President and President, Books and Education Publishing; Ericka Markman, President, Children's Books and Education Publishing Group; Nancy Feresten, Vice President, Children's Books, Editor-in-Chief; Steve Mico, Vice President Education Publishing Group, Editorial Director; Marianne Hiland, Editorial Manager; Anita Schwartz, Project Editor; Tara Peterson, Editorial Assistant; Jim Hiscott, Design Manager; Linda McKnight, Art Director; Diana Bourdrez, Anne Whittle, Photo Research; Matt Wascavage, Manager of Publishing Services; Sean Philpotts, Production Coordinator; Jane Ponton, Production Artist; Susan Donnelly, Children's Books Project Editor. Production: Clifton M. Brown III, Manufacturing and Quality Control.

PROGRAM DEVELOPMENT
Gare Thompson Associates, Inc.

CONSULTANTS/REVIEWERS
Dr. Margit E. McGuire, School of Education, Seattle University, Seattle, Washington

BOOK DESIGN
Steven Curtis Design, Inc.

NATIONAL GEOGRAPHIC SOCIETY
1145 17th Street, N.W.
Washington, D.C. 20036-4688

Printed in Mexico

Table of Contents

"Only recently… have we come to realize that what Columbus did in 1492 was to link two old worlds, thereby creating one new world."

~Herman J. Viola, Curator,
Smithsonian Museums

Introduction

Nearly 500 years ago, Christopher Columbus sailed from Spain in search of a trade route to the riches of Asia. He landed instead in the Americas. European explorers who followed thought that they had discovered a New World. What they had really discovered was a world that was new to them.

Native Americans had been living in the lands they thought were "new" for over 10,000 years. By the time of the arrival of the Europeans in the late 1400s, there were hundreds of Native American **cultures** in the Americas. These cultures spoke different languages and lived in different ways. Some Native Americans lived in large cities. Others were farmers who lived in small villages. Still others were hunters and gatherers. They moved when they needed more food.

Many of the tools and resources the explorers brought with them from Europe were unfamiliar to Native Americans. Likewise, many Native American resources and tools were new to Europeans. Contact between these two cultures would change life in the Americas forever.

Christopher Columbus

CHAPTER 1

Different Cultures Different Ways

On August 3, 1492, Christopher Columbus set sail from Spain with three small ships. After months at sea, with the crew ready to return home, a sailor finally spotted land on October 12. Within a few hours, the ships were anchored on an island in the Caribbean Columbus named "San Salvador." Thinking he had landed in a part of Asia called the Indies, Columbus called the people he met Indians. Actually, the people Columbus met were Taino.

The Taino lived differently than the explorers. They traveled in canoes instead of sailing ships. They grew cotton, tobacco, and foods such as corn, yams, pineapple, and a starchy root called manioc. They also ate fish, shellfish, sea turtles, and iguanas. Columbus and his men had never seen many of these foods. They were used to pigs, cattle, chickens, wheat, and rice.

The Taino lived in a hot climate so they did not need much clothing. The Spaniards wore lots of clothing, shoes, and even armor! The Spaniards had weapons such as guns and cannons. They came from a country that had been fighting wars over land and power for many years.

The two cultures differed in other ways as well. They spoke different languages. They also had different **values**, or things that were important to them. Their differences made it hard for them to understand each other.

The Taino and many other Native American tribes gave gifts to visitors. It was their way of showing friendship and respect. The Taino chief gave Columbus gold and parrots. Columbus gave him glass beads and brass bells. To the Taino, the exchange of gifts was a symbol of friendship. Columbus misunderstood. He thought the Taino did not care about owning things.

Columbus claimed the land he discovered for Spain. He returned to the Americas three more times bringing with him settlers and supplies. The settlers raised the same foods they ate in Europe. Without knowing it, Columbus also brought weeds, rats, and European diseases.

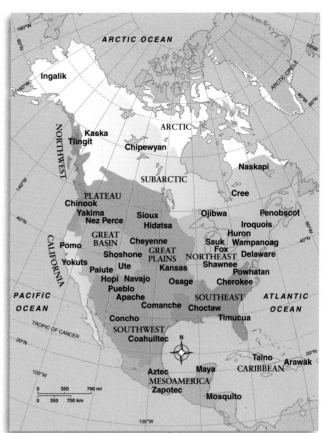

NATIVE AMERICAN CULTURAL REGIONS, 1500

VOICES FROM AMERICA

"Of anything they have, if you ask them for it, they never say no. Rather they invite the person to share it, and show as much love as if they were giving their hearts . . . they are content with whatever little thing of whatever kind may be given to them."

~ *Christopher Columbus, writing about the Taino*

Native American Ways of Life

Before Europeans came to North America, Native Americans traded with each other and learned from one another. The Pueblo, for example, taught the Navajo how to farm.

Different tribes had different ways of life, but all Native Americans respected the earth. Some tribes, such as the Iroquois, had thanksgiving ceremonies when their crops ripened. Others, such as the Abenaki, apologized to an animal when they killed it. They used all of its meat. They thought these actions helped an animal species to survive. In turn, the Abenaki would always have food.

Most Native Americans used storytelling to keep their history. A few tribes had a system of writing. Some tribes kept records using pictures drawn on animal skins or bark. Others used **wampum**, or beads made from shells. Most depended on their memory to keep traditions alive. They sang songs, told folktales, and shared poetry. The stories entertained and informed people. Children learned how to behave by listening to stories. Other stories told how things were created or happened.

▼ Pueblo built this adobe village in Taos, New Mexico, over 1,000 years ago.

Native American Homes

Homes varied from region to region. Native Americans built homes with materials in their environment. Native Americans living on the plains where there were few trees built homes out of **sod**, grass-covered soil held together by roots. The Pawnee dug their homes partway into the ground. They used wooden supports and finished their homes with layers of branches, sod, and mud.

In the Southwest, the Pueblo often used **adobe**, or clay bricks, to build villages. Pueblo homes had many stories, just like apartment buildings. The Pueblo entered their homes through a hole in the roof. They used a ladder to get to the roof. They kept safe by pulling the ladder up behind them. Some Pueblo built villages along cliffs or on top of **mesas**, flat-topped mountains.

The Iroquois of the Northeast lived in longhouses. Many families, all related, lived in one longhouse. Each family had its own part of the longhouse. The Iroquois built their homes with wood and shingles of elm bark.

▲ **Algonquians built homes with pole frameworks and roofs covered with bark.**

Riches

At the time Columbus sailed to the Americas, European countries were competing with each for new lands and new trade routes. The country with the most land and riches would become the most powerful.

After Columbus, other Europeans set out to explore the Americas. Amerigo Vespucci was among the first to realize that he was exploring places that were new to Europeans. European mapmakers called the newly discovered lands "America" in his honor.

▲ Hernán Cortés

Spanish **conquistadores,** such as Hernán Cortés, came to find gold and silver. Cortés was successful. He received gold and valuable gifts from the Aztec ruler. The Aztecs were a powerful Native American people who lived in Mexico. Cortés wanted to conquer the Aztecs and claim their land for Spain. He had guns, which the Aztecs had never seen. He also brought over European diseases that killed many Aztecs. Within two years, Cortés had destroyed the Aztec empire.

Other Europeans went to the Americas to fish, hunt, and trap animals for fur. They cut down forests for wood and farmland.

MEET AZTEC WARRIORS AND SPANISH CONQUISTADORES

Aztec warriors and Spanish conquistadores had different ideas about keeping clean. From about 1400–1700, few Europeans bathed regularly. Instead, some people used paint and powder to cover up dirt and perfume to hide body odor. The Aztecs, on the other hand, understood that keeping clean was one way to stay healthy. They bathed often and even took steam baths. The Aztecs cleaned their teeth regularly with powdered charcoal and salt, an early form of toothpaste.

Europe in the 1600s

By 1600, many European countries had set up **colonies** in different parts of the world, including North America. A colony gave a country a way to get more land and wealth. Colonists spent money to buy goods from their home country. They also shipped goods, such as crops and furs, back home.

Farming was important in Europe, but farmers often were poor. In some countries, rich people owned much of the land. It was difficult for a poor person to buy farmland. America had lots of unspoiled land that could be turned into farmland. Some people came to America because they wanted land. For them, owning land was a sign of success. Others came to America to practice their religion freely.

In 1620, the Pilgrims set sail from England to America aboard the *Mayflower*.

11

First Impressions

Many Native Americans welcomed Europeans at first. Others had heard about the Europeans before they met them. They heard that Europeans kidnapped Native Americans and destroyed their villages. So, some Native Americans ran away from Europeans. They fired arrows to scare them away.

Europeans did many things that were against Native American ways. Trappers ruined hunting grounds. They caught hundreds of animals. Often they took only their fur. Native Americans killed only what they needed. They used the entire animal.

Settlers claimed land as their own. This idea of private property was strange to most Native Americans. They believed that everyone could use the land. Land ownership caused much fighting between settlers and Native Americans.

Europeans tried to force other parts of their culture on Native Americans. Missionaries tried to **convert** some Native Americans to Christianity.

CHAPTER 2

New Harvests, New Foods

In spite of the conflicts between Native Americans and Europeans, the two cultures learned many things from one another. They learned about new foods and crops. Europeans brought seeds for many of their favorite foods to the Americas, but many settlers could not wait for the seeds to grow. They had to eat new foods or they would starve to death. The Native Americans introduced the settlers to many new foods.

Native Americans and settlers also learned new ways of preparing foods from one another. For instance, Europeans were introduced to pemmican, a Native American food made from dried meat mixed with berries. This was a good food to take on long journeys because it did not spoil easily.

Native Americans also showed settlers where and how to fish and hunt. They taught settlers better ways of planting. Squanto, a Native American, showed the Pilgrims how to plant corn. He also taught them to fertilize their crops with dead fish.

Corn

Corn, or **maize**, was the most important food grown by Native Americans. Scientists think corn was first grown in Peru and Mexico. It quickly spread through other parts of North America. Corn could be eaten boiled or roasted on the cob. It could be dried and ground into cornmeal. Native Americans even made popcorn! They also made corn dumplings and soup. Southeastern Native Americans ground and boiled corn to make a dish called grits. They taught European colonists to make grits. Grits is still a favorite food in many parts of the United States.

Corn also became one of the most important crops grown by the European settlers. Native Americans in the Northeast taught the settlers how to plant corn. They used a system called hilling. First they formed small hills of dirt in rows. Then they planted a corn kernel in each hill. Planting corn this way was much better than the European way. Europeans threw seeds onto the ground. Birds and other animals saw the seeds and quickly ate them. By covering seeds with dirt, crops had a better chance to grow.

▼ A Mexican farmer harvests ears of corn.

The Three Sisters

Many Native Americans planted squash, beans, and corn together. They called the plants the Three Sisters. Planting the crops together took up less space in a garden. Beans twisted up the cornstalks. The squash choked weeds and kept the soil moist. The plants helped each other grow better.

▲ "The Three Sisters," a watercolor by a Seneca artist, Ernest Smith

Maple Syrup and Sugar

The Native Americans of the Northeast showed the colonists how to make maple syrup. First they tapped the maple trees during the first warm days of spring. Sap from the trees dripped into a bucket. Then they boiled the sap until it turned into syrup. Early European explorers described the syrup as "sweet water." If the syrup boiled long enough, it turned into maple sugar.

The Spanish had brought sugarcane to the Americas. They grew it on **plantations**, very large farms, in the Caribbean. By the mid-1700s, sugarcane was also being grown in the South. Many people were needed to work on the plantations. So, Europeans traders brought back to America shiploads of Africans captured by West African rulers and merchants and sold as slaves.

Slave traders often took a route that was triangle-shaped. Ships carried goods from New England to western Africa. In Africa, the goods were traded for slaves. Then the ships sailed to the West Indies, where the slaves were sold. There the traders bought sugar, molasses, and other goods. Finally, they sailed back to New England to sell their last load of goods.

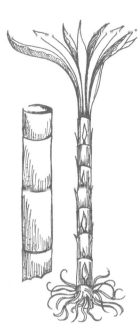

▲ Sugarcane

▼ Collecting sap from maple trees

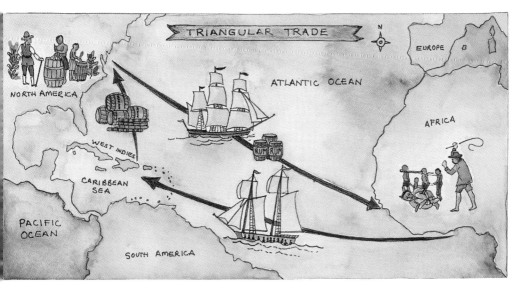

Cash Crops

The American colonists learned about two other crops from the Native Americans. They were cotton and tobacco, which soon became important **cash crops** for the colonists. Farmers sold most of these crops instead of using them. Often, the farmers became wealthy.

English colonists saw Native Americans use tobacco in important ceremonies. Soon, Europeans were smoking tobacco, too. They learned how to make clay pipes much like the ones the Native Americans used. Then the Europeans began planting tobacco on plantations. Tobacco helped Virginia and other colonies become rich. Colonists began to plant more and more tobacco.

Settlers also grew cotton on plantations. They grew Native American cotton. Its long fibers made it excellent for weaving. Native Americans had been weaving beautiful cloth long before Europeans came to the Americas.

Cotton and tobacco plantations were so large that they needed lots of workers. Most of those workers were slaves. By 1750, about 200,000 slaves lived in the 13 American colonies. Most of them worked on plantations in the South. By 1860, the number of slaves in the South had grown to about four million.

▲ **Tobacco plant**

Native American Animals

Europeans saw some animals they did not recognize when they reached North America. These animals included wild turkey and buffalo. Wild turkey lived in most of America. Early Spanish explorers had brought some turkeys back to Spain. People liked the tasty birds. Soon, turkeys became a popular food throughout much of Europe. The Pilgrims even brought turkeys from England to America to raise for food. They did not know that turkeys ran wild in Massachusetts.

The American elk, a type of deer, roamed much of the United States and southern Canada. Native Americans hunted them. Soon Europeans did, too. They hunted thousands of elk. After a time, elk could only be found west of the Rocky Mountains.

About 50 million buffalo once roamed the North American Plains. The Plains Indians used the buffalo for food, clothing, shelter, tools, fuel, and medicine. European settlers hunted the buffalo, too. Often they hunted for sport or they took the skins and left the meat to rot in the sun. Settlers killed millions of buffalo. By 1889, fewer than 600 buffalo remained in the United States. The Plains Indians had to change their way of life. Too few buffalo remained to support the Plains Indians.

▼ "Buffalo Herd Grazing," a painting by George Catlin

European Animals

Europeans brought different kinds of animals to the Americas. Among these animals were pigs, cattle, goats, and sheep.

Pigs became a good food for Native Americans and settlers. However, pigs destroyed many plants and animals that were native to the Americas. Pigs trampled grasses. And how they ate! They dug roots and vegetables out of the ground. They gobbled up baby birds, eggs, fruits, and vegetables. They even ate shellfish!

Nothing seemed to stop them. If the sun was too hot, the pigs crawled under bushes or into a hole. One Spanish explorer reported that in 16 years his herd of pigs had increased from 24 to 30,000! Pigs were soon running wild.

Cattle, sheep, and goats also did well in the Americas. In 1598, Spanish colonists marched into New Mexico along with their herds of cattle, sheep, and goats. The colonists forced the Pueblo Indians to work for them. The work included taking care of the animals.

Raising Animals

The Spanish taught the Pueblo how to raise animals. The Pueblo passed these skills on to many Navajo. Sheep, goats, and cattle became a new part of the Native American diet. Goats produced milk to be made into cheese and butter.

The Pueblo and Navajo also used the wool from sheep. They spun the wool and dyed it with plants. Then they wove it into clothing and blankets. Raising animals and weaving became important work for many Native Americans.

Sheep and goats were especially suited to the climate of the Southwest. They could live on the dry, tough plants that grew there. Cattle did well in the rich pastures of the grasslands.

Rats also made their way to the Americas. They stowed away in ships. Then they scrambled or swam ashore. Rats were new to the Americas, too. Like pigs, they did well. They ate nearly everything. They destroyed crops and ate stored foods. They carried diseases.

One animal, however, would change forever how the Native Americans lived. It was the horse.

◄ A Navajo woman shears sheep.

CHAPTER 3

The Horse: Changing Lifestyles

Some Native Americans were amazed when they first saw a horse. Others were terrified. The Aztecs described a Spaniard on a horse as a man-animal. They thought the horse and rider were one animal. They were amazed when the rider got off the horse.

Some Native Americans called the horse "big dog." Others called it "sky dog." They thought it was a monster. Still others called the horse "elk dog" because it was the same size as an elk. This confusing animal changed the way of life of many Native Americans. It changed the way they traveled, hunted, and fought.

Some Native Americans believe that the horse was always in America. Most scientists disagree. They think that the horse arrived in America more than 40 million years ago. Then, horses crossed a land bridge from Alaska into Siberia. From there, they spread to Europe. Somehow, the horses that remained in America died out. They may have been eaten by other animals. No one is sure what happened. But thousands of years later, Columbus brought them back to the Americas.

The Horse Arrives in America

Some Native Americans living in the Southeast first saw horses when Spanish explorers came to Florida and the Carolinas in the 1500s. Most Native Americans in North America, however, did not see a horse until 1598. That was the year a band of Spanish colonists settled in New Mexico. Among the animals they brought to New Mexico were horses.

Over time, the Native Americans watched how the Spaniards treated their animals. They learned how to care for the horses. They also learned how to ride. The Spaniards had bridles and saddles for their horses, but many Native Americans learned to ride without either. They soon became skilled riders. Warriors rode their horses in battle. They could hide themselves by slipping to one side of the animal. That way, their horse became a galloping shield!

In 1680, the Pueblo revolted against the settlers in New Mexico. Many of the settlers fled. They left their animals behind. Native Americans kept some horses. Other horses ran wild. They formed herds that spread north into the Plains. Soon, other Native Americans would be riding.

The Navajo and the Horse

Before the Navajo had horses, they traveled, fought, and hunted on foot. Once they had horses, they could do all these things on horseback. It became important for men and boys to ride well.

Horses could travel faster and farther than people. Now, the Navajo could go farther to trade because their horses could carry heavy bundles of goods. It became important to have many horses. More horses could carry more goods.

With horses, the Navajo had more choices about where to live. They could live farther away from water and their farms. Their horses could carry heavy water bags to their homes.

Horses also changed the way Navajo warriors fought. On horseback, the Navajo could strike swiftly and leave quickly. Thanks to the horse, few Spanish colonists wanted to settle on Navajo land.

The Plains Indians Before the Horse

The horse also changed the Plains Indians' way of life. Before they had horses, many Plains Indians lived in villages along rivers. Their houses were earth lodges. In the summer, the men lived on the Plains to hunt buffalo. Their summer homes were **tipis** made of animal skins.

Hunting buffalo on foot was hard and dangerous work. Sometimes, hunters covered themselves with animal skins. Slowly, they crept up to the grazing buffalo. Then they hurled their spears. Other times, hunters tried to make the buffalo run off a cliff, so they would be easier to kill. A third way to hunt buffalos was to light a circle of fire around a grazing herd. The animals would trample each other, or they might suffocate from the smoke. In any case, a hunter could be killed or wounded by the hoofs or horns of stampeding buffalo.

The Plains Indians After the Horse

By the end of the 1600s, the horse had spread to the northern Plains. Tribes of the eastern Plains still lived in earth lodges. The horse made it easy for the Plains Indians to reach the buffalo herds quickly. Their horses could pull buffalo back to the village.

Tribes living on the western Plains no longer lived in earth lodges. These Native Americans became year-round buffalo hunters. Large tipis became their homes. Horses pulled the tipis from camp to camp.

Now that buffalo was so much easier to hunt, buffalo skins became the main material for clothing. Buffalo hides were also used for bedding and tipis. Buffalo meat became the main food. Native Americans dried buffalo meat in the sun to preserve it. It tasted good and lasted a long time. They made tools from the horns and bones. They used dried buffalo manure, called buffalo chips, as fuel.

▼ Carl F. Wimar, The Buffalo Hunt, 1860. Oil on canvas, 35 $\frac{1}{4}$ x 60". Washington University Gallery of Art, St. Louis. Gift of Dr. William van Zandt, 1886.

Other Life Changes

With a horse, hunting took much less time. As a result, Plains Indians had more time to do other things. Women spent more time sewing costumes for ceremonial dances. Men often spent time raiding other tribes for horses and supplies. They also protected their families and homes from attack by settlers or other tribes.

Some tribes were pushed farther west as settlers took their land. As one tribe moved, it pushed other tribes off their hunting grounds. Many of these relocated tribes, such as the Sioux and the Comanche, began to use the horse.

▼ "Wedding Ceremony," a painting by Kiowa artist, Steve Mopope

Some Native American tribes continued to farm. Often, they were attacked by warring horse-riding Native Americans who stole their crops. Soon, even some farming tribes, such as the Cheyenne, adopted the horse.

The horse brought still other changes. It made trade easier. Horses could carry heavy loads and travel long distances. Native American tribes who had never before met were now trading.

CHAPTER 4

Trade

Trading was important to Native Americans and to settlers alike. By the time the Europeans arrived in the Americas, Native Americans were trading with one another. Often trade routes followed waterways.

Scientists have discovered that many of the materials that Native Americans used to make objects came from long distances. For example, Native Americans living as far away as Canada, Texas, Maine, and California used a red stone from Minnesota to make pipes. As a result, many scientists think that Native Americans may have traveled long distances from their homes to trade. Also, goods may have been traded over shorter distances from one trader to the next until the goods reached a tribe far away.

▼ **"Indian Encampment on Lake Huron,"** a painting by Paul Kane

Usually, goods were **bartered**, or exchanged. The two sides doing the trading would agree on the worth of the objects. Then the objects would be exchanged. For example, a basket might be exchanged for a bundle of corn.

Trading Among Native Americans

Native Americans traded many goods with one another. Freshwater pearls and stones that could be easily carved were prized trade items. Another prized item was **obsidian**—a dark, hard, glassy, volcanic rock—used to make arrowheads, spear points, and other sharp tools. Much obsidian came from the Rocky Mountains. Also valued were metals such as copper and silver for making tools and ornaments.

In the Southwest, some Navajo traded with Pueblo villages. They traded meat, hides, and stone tools for Pueblo cloth, pottery, corn, beans, and squash. Other Native Americans of the Southwest traded goods for shells from the Gulf of California. They made jewelry from the shells.

Native Americans who lived along the seacoast used shells to trade with tribes who lived far from the ocean. Large shells were prized as tools, ornaments, and ceremonial objects. Turtle shells from the Gulf of Mexico were also traded. They were used to make jewelry and other decorations.

Trading with the French

Native Americans traded with the French as well. The French came to North America looking for fish and furs, especially beaver furs. By 1600, the beaver had nearly died out in Europe. North America seemed to have an endless supply of them. To find furs, the French needed the help of Native American guides and **interpreters,** people who could speak both Native American languages and French. These experts knew the trade routes and the trading partners.

▲ A trader shows Native Americans cloth and other goods produced in Europe.

Native Americans began trading beaver furs for metal, cloth, and guns. Sometimes, they traded for mirrors or beads. Native Americans did not have iron or guns. Therefore, they wanted knives, axes, hatchets, guns, and even kettles. The French were happy to trade these things for beaver furs.

When hunters had trapped all the beaver in one area, they moved to another. Soon, Native American hunters were wiping out entire beaver populations. They were also disturbing other tribes' hunting. Fighting soon broke out between Native American tribes. The French were part of these battles, too.

THE POPULAR BEAVER

The beaver was probably hunted more than any other animal in North America from the late 1500s through 1800. Both settlers and Native Americans ate beaver meat. They also traded its fur which was used to make hats, coats, and other items of clothing. In the late 1600s, one rifle could buy five beaver skins. Lots of beavers were trapped. By the late 1800s, few beavers remained in North America.

Trading with Other Europeans

WORD ORIGINS

Many Native American words became part of the English language. See if you recognize any of these words.

hammock (from Taino): a hanging bed made of notted cord

moccasin (from Algonquian): a soft leather slipper

powwow (from Narragansett): a meeting or council

squash (from Narragansett): fleshy fruit related to the pumpkin

toboggan (from Algonquian): a long, flat-bottom sled

The Dutch and English wanted furs, too. The Iroquois traded furs for guns. The Dutch discovered that the Iroquois valued wampum most of all and so the Dutch began to trade wampum for furs.

The Navajo traded with the Spaniards. The Navajo traded baskets, pottery, and foods for iron axes, knives, and pots. They also traded for cotton and wool cloth. As a result of trading with the Europeans, Native Americans began to use new designs and materials in their crafts. For example, Native American women began decorating the clothing they made with glass beads bought from European traders. They also began to weave European designs, such as patterns of flowers. Some Native Americans carved pipes with European faces.

Disease

Goods weren't the only things that passed along trade routes. Diseases did, too. Many Native Americans died from diseases brought to America by the Europeans. Some historians estimate that 50 to 90 percent of Native Americans died from European diseases. Even the common cold killed Native Americans when they were first exposed to the disease.

No one knows the exact number of Taino who lived in the Caribbean when Columbus arrived. Their population has been estimated from 60,000 to eight million. By 1600, the Taino were gone. Most of them had died from smallpox.

Smallpox was a dreadful disease. It sometimes wiped out entire villages. Many settlers were protected from smallpox. They had the disease as children.

VOICES FROM AMERICA

"[The Indians] are astonished and often complain that, since the French mingle with them and carry on trade with them, they are dying fast and the population is thinning out. . . . they tell how one by one the different coasts, according as they have begun to traffic with us [the French] have been reduced by disease."

~ *from a 1616 issue of Jesuit Relations*

In addition to smallpox, bubonic plague, scarlet fever, typhus, cholera, measles, and diphtheria spread through the Americas. Fleas and rats spread some of these diseases. Other diseases spread when a sick person came into contact with a healthy person. Some diseases spread when a healthy person handled an object covered with germs.

One story tells of some Blackfeet scouts who came to a Shoshone Village. They saw horses grazing, but they didn't see any people. When they looked in the tipis, they saw that everyone had died. The Shoshone had died of smallpox. The scouts looted the camp and returned to their village. Within weeks, two-thirds of the Blackfeet tribe had died. The looted objects had smallpox germs on them. By handling them, the Blackfeet got the disease, too.

Native Americans soon began to suspect that Europeans caused many of the diseases. They noticed that their people became ill after having contact with Europeans. Many Native Americans saw the settlers as the destroyers of the Native Americans.

CHAPTER 5

Changing Ways of Life

Europeans and Native Americans learned many important things from one another. They learned new ways to do things.

Europeans learned better ways of planting. They tried planting crops that were new to them. Then they sent these new foods to Europe. Many Native American crops, such as potatoes, grew better in Europe than did European crops. Today, many Native American foods—such as yams, corn, and peanuts—are grown around the world.

European crops, products, and animals became important to Native Americans, too. The horse became a major part of Native American life and legends. Crops such as wheat spread across America. Today, North America is one of the world's biggest producers of wheat.

Europeans and Native Americans learned other things, too. They learned new ways to build, travel, and play.

Fighting Hunger and Disease

Native Americans used many different plants to heal wounds and cure illnesses. Even so, few European settlers thought that Native American healers had any medical knowledge. Actually, Native Americans knew a lot about plants and healing. Native Americans made one medicine to cure headaches and other pains. It was made from willow leaves and willow bark. Today, scientists know that aspirin is based on some of the same ingredients.

Scientists have also discovered that some Native American foods have nutritional value. One Native American food rich in minerals and proteins is amaranth. It tastes like spinach. Like corn, it can be ground into flour and used to bake bread and make pancakes.

Another Native American food is quinoa, a grain that grows in Peru, Colorado, and New Mexico. It is a good source of protein. People add quinoa to stews, soups, salads, and even cooked cereals.

Amaranth

Arts

Native Americans made containers to carry things. They made containers in different sizes, depending on their purpose. Native Americans and settlers often traded goods for these containers.

Some cultures were know for their embroidered pouches. Others were known for their pottery. Some, such as the Pueblo and Maidu, wove beautiful baskets. Maidu women gathered materials to make the baskets. Whenever they took something from nature, they put another thing in its place. That way, they would not upset the balance of the earth.

Maidu women could make watertight baskets for carrying water. They could even use their baskets to boil water! The women had a special way to make watertight baskets. They also wove a special design into each basket. When it was finished, the basket was not only practical. It was a work of art as well!

Today, people around the world admire the skilled work of Native American artists. Many people collect their baskets, pottery, and other crafts.

Architecture

The two cultures learned much about building from each other. Native Americans began to use metal tools, such as nails, in their buildings. They also used paint, wooden boards, and bricks.

The first European settlers on the Great Plains built sod houses. They were much like the earth lodges of the Plains Indians. They stayed cool in summer and warm in winter.

Spanish settlers learned to make adobe bricks and build their homes with them. Today, many modern buildings in America, especially in the West and Southwest, look like Pueblo homes. Algonquians and Iroquois built a circle of tall, thick posts around their villages. European settlers built similar fences, called **stockades**, around their settlements. Later, settlers turned their stockades into wooden forts. People still fence in their yards with stockade-like fences.

Travel and Games

Many Europeans used Native American means of transportation to get around. The French explored American waterways in canoes. The canoes were easier to use than the heavy French boats. Some canoes were made from birch bark. That made them light. If a river became too shallow, a canoe could be carried easily.

Native Americans showed Europeans how to make snowshoes. Snowshoes kept people from sinking into deep snow. Toboggans were another Native American invention. Toboggans helped people get around or move things across the snow.

Native Americans played many games. One of them was lacrosse. It is still played around the world. Lacrosse is a team sport. Players move the ball with their sticks. They try to score goals by throwing the ball into the other team's goal.

▼ "Ball Play," a painting by George Catlin

Different Beliefs

Most Native Americans saw themselves as caretakers of the earth. They did not believe in owning land. Everyone could use the earth's resources, but certain rules had to be followed. People should never take more than they needed. They should not be wasteful. When they took something, they should give something back. For example, a hunter might leave part of his catch for forest animals to eat.

European settlers had different beliefs. Most of them wanted to own land. They wanted to turn it into farms or ranches. Owning land was a sign of wealth. Most settlers did not understand that nature must be cared for. They thought that the earth's natural resources, such as forests, would last forever.

These different ideas about land use resulted in conflicts between Native Americans and settlers. Land-hungry settlers built farms and towns on Native American hunting grounds. They destroyed Native American villages and forced some cultures to move onto reservations and change their way of life.

Today, people are paying more attention to protecting the earth's resources. Many lumber companies plant trees after they cut down a forest. People are cleaning up the water. Companies are trying to do less harm to the environment.

We still can learn many things from the past. We can learn better ways of treating one another. We can learn to respect cultures different from our own. We can learn better ways of listening to the earth.

Glossary

adobe clay bricks

barter to exchange one thing for another without using money

cash crop a crop, such as tobacco or cotton, grown to be sold for profit

colony a territory that is ruled by another country

conquistador one who conquers; Spanish conqueror of the Americas

convert to convince someone to change his or her beliefs

culture the arts, beliefs, and customs that make up a way of life for a group of people

interpreter someone who translates one language into another

maize corn

mesa flat-topped mountain

obsidian volcanic glass, usually black

plantation a very large farm on which crops such as cotton and sugarcane are grown

sod grass-covered soil held together by roots

stockade a fence made of strong posts set upright in the ground

tipi a tent shaped like a cone

values things that are important to people

wampum beads made from shells strung together and used by Native Americans as money

INDEX